I0233626

What Has Been Left Behind

What Has Been Left Behind

Cole William Hartin

RESOURCE *Publications* · Eugene, Oregon

WHAT HAS BEEN LEFT BEHIND

Copyright © 2024 Cole William Hartin. All rights reserved. Except for brief quotations in critical publications or reviews, no part of this book may be reproduced in any manner without prior written permission from the publisher. Write: Permissions, Wipf and Stock Publishers, 199 W. 8th Ave., Suite 3, Eugene, OR 97401.

Resource Publications
An Imprint of Wipf and Stock Publishers
199 W. 8th Ave., Suite 3
Eugene, OR 97401

www.wipfandstock.com

PAPERBACK ISBN: 979-8-3852-0604-9
HARDCOVER ISBN: 979-8-3852-0605-6
EBOOK ISBN: 979-8-3852-0606-3

VERSION NUMBER 012324

To Amy, with all of my love.

Contents

Preface

Poetry, for me, has been a means of staying alive. And by that, I don't mean to say that poetry has saved me from dying—though I think good poetry (or even bad poetry, for that matter) has such power. But I mean to say that poetry has kept my heart alive in a season of life when it would have been easy for it to start to die. I have in mind the global convulsions of the past few years especially, but also some personal situations that have been trying.

Most of these poems have been shaped by the coastline of southern New Brunswick, where I had the privilege to live for about five years. This was a deeply formative time for me, and this rugged and beautiful place was something more like a character in my life than a mere setting. Saint John remains the place I wish I was from. The Bay of Fundy, and the Wolastoq (St. John) River are sources of deep mystery and joy. Life has taken me to the Piney Woods of East Texas. I am grateful to be here, and for the kind people who share their life with me. Still, I remember what has been left behind.

As much as the foggy coast shaped these poems, so did my struggle to be a faithful priest and pastor. The vocation to a life of poetry has not been unrelated to the spiritual life. Despite the challenges that come with both, I am thankful to a have this yoke around my neck.

Acknowledgements

I AM GRATEFUL TO many people for the opportunity to write this book.

First, for the conversation and encouragement of Malcom Guite, in Oxford at The Descent of the Dove conference at Pusey House, and then this past year during his course "Lifting the Veil: Imagination and the Kingdom of God" at Nashotah House. A group of us gathered around Guite, and he rambled through clouds of pipe smoke. He seemed to be just talking off the top of his head, but his ideas opened a window for me.

I want to thank the kind people who have published my poems that reappear in this volume:

Sections of "Movements in the Fog" first appeared in *Montréal Writes*. February 2020

"Holy Week", "An Afternoon Run", "Storm Surge", and "The Beach" all first appeared in *The Nashwaak Review*. Volume 44/45, Issue 1, Fall/Winter 2020/21: p. 159–161.

Parts of the "Birthing Suite" first appeared in *The Antigonish Review*. Volume 51, Issues 205–206, Spring/Summer 2021: pp. 104–5.

"On Childhood" first appeared in *The Amethyst Review*. August 28, 2021.

"The Stones" and "The Fog Again" first appeared in *The Reformed Journal*. March 7, 2023.

"Picking Strawberries in the Fog" and "The Fly" both appeared in *Ekstasis Magazine*, in the 2023 Winter Collection and Spring Collection, respectively.

Many of these poems have been birthed out of experiences in pastoral ministry. Thanks to the parishioners of St. Luke's, Parish of Portland, and to the good folks of Christ Church, Tyler.

I want to thank my faithful friend David Adkins for his willingness to read this manuscript.

I am grateful for my parents, Brenda and Larry, and to my parents-in-law, Barb and Steve.

I am grateful to my four sons, Ambrose, Isaac, Ephraim, and August. Together they've introduced a joy (with a little grief) into my life that has often spurred me to write. These poems would not exist without them.

Finally, thanks to Amy for her encouragement and love.

The Warming

On the Spring

I had a dream from that time when
we were students, walking
up the hill on one Pacific spring.
My legs ached from the incline as you
talked over birdsong and the breath
of cherry blossoms.

The weather was fair, milder
than I expected
having grown up in
steely Eastern climes.
All of the verdant greens were illuminated,
the sky was royal blue.
(Do you remember that blue?)
Our whole lives stretched out
before us like the forest and the
hills.

The Surface

At last the morning cracks open
with the sun's rays spilling over the horizon,
a welcome sight after days of gray and nights
of blue.

The river teems with wind
above and currents under

its surface.
This is all I know:

The thin, visible line where water meets
air, from which liquid turns to vapor.

The is all I know.

The depths are a mystery
and so are the heights of the expanse.
I see only where they meet,
I see only the teeming waters.

Adjusting

Car rumble and computer hum, the
ticking of my watch. These sounds
replace what I once knew as silence.
Mechanical beats strangle nature's breath.

But I see fewer bugs, hear less of the
whine of insect wings. I sweat less, and the thermostat
reminds me I have no need to shiver.

Yet, I miss the sound of ocean and the old cold land,
despite all its faults. I wish I missed the pain too, but
homesickness is just as much a mirage as a longing.

Better life, better life, better life.

Picking Strawberries in the Fog

We awoke in a cloud
and, after drinking our coffee,
mustered our children,
shepherding them into their car seats.
We punched a tunnel through the fog in
our minivan.

We left the fluorescent orbs behind with
the city, our path not much lightened
by the muted rays of sun.

Patches of dense fog lifted to unveil
leaden skies and beside us the
verdant green of full summer
well-watered.

We climbed the hill to the
strawberry field, all the while
overlooking the river and its rising banks.
They disappeared into the clouds so that
I could have believed they kept climbing,
kept rising into real mountains, instead of
these worn-down Appalachian hills.

I thought this looked like some imagined
ancestral homeland, like a place I wish
I was from.

We picked (and ate) our fill, each of us,
syrupy juice dripping from the corners of our mouths,
some running down my beard, running onto my jacket, onto
the collar of my jacket.

I paid the smiling lady with my
dirty money before we rode home
in near silence.

Crash

The accident on the bridge this summer
slowed all of us down.
The flashing harsh lights signaled trouble,
as did the jagged, twisted metal.
We stared, gawking at the calamity.

Some honked horns.
I rolled my eyes,
and rehearsed ways to explain
my late arrival.
What an inconvenience it is
to have someone injured.

Or dead.

Does the soul leave the body when a car crash flings it to concrete?
Like a helicopter, or a drone,
does the spirit ascend above the harbor and the bridge?
I wonder how high it goes.

On Waiting

I've let my heart lay fallow these last few days
in hopes that the barrenness will sprout forth
a few shoots.

Seeds scattered very long ago,
gifts of memory, like the lush emerald grass in my
backyard when I was growing up, or,
walking around in the freezing cold with friends
on dark nights just before Christmas.

What other phantasms haunt my mind?
How many remain lost to memory?

For these past three years I've been trying to coax
some new growth out of depleted soil,
straining each day to see any difference.
There's been very little green, only
brittle shoots that dry up before long.

So here I am in this sabbath rest,
letting my heart lie fallow, letting my mind wander,
and my legs too, when I can find the time.

Maybe I will see a new leaf. Maybe not.

Holy Week

The roads and the sidewalks
are littered with garbage:
coffee cups, old shingles,
beer cans, and all kinds of
other debris.

It's springtime, of course,
and when the snow
has melted, the detritus
is what we find.

There is more in the park across the street:
Dog excrement, shredded plastic bags,
and an old mattress, soaking, rotting,
under the lonely birch.

Wednesday in Holy Week and
I scan for signs of hope amidst
the evidence of negligence and decay.
The river flows as it always does,
rising and falling with the tide,
toxic with jetsam we've hurled with
careless indifference.

I've been biting my nails, chewing
my cuticles, feeling the pain,
watching the drip of blood.
Is this more pollution or the tortures of penitence?

Storm Surge

I'm cast loose upon the waves of time
like those waves we watched on Good Friday
pounding against the parking lot
much higher than we've come to know
because of the storm surge.

We let our children watch these waves,
but not be carried off by them.
We keep watch,
as they bash against the stairs and leap
higher still.
(The waves, I mean, not my children.)

I can't keep watch very long over my kin,
or over my wandering mind.
I've allowed it to drift on
the waves of time but now
I cannot reel it in.

I smell salt spray and listen
to the gull's vulturous cries.

The Beach

My life is like that broken bottle
I found on the beach.
Glass smashed, what was left of it.
No longer capable of carrying beer
or sea water, unable
to keep itself together.

Broken glass is dangerous
especially around small children
and little dogs.
It's apt to cut into exposed flesh.

But the tide will come in,
oh, yes, the tide will come in.
And it will bear the broken bottle and its
fragments away.

Over months and weeks
these jagged edges will blunt and
dull and be transfigured as if by some
unrelenting prayer.
They will become an interesting specimen,
a curiosity to beachcombers,
one small relic of beauty.

An Afternoon Run

The wind is unceasing and
I feel it in my sweat, in my bones,
as I pound the sidewalk by the park
along the bay.

It's spring, and the sun warms my beard,
then the icy wind cuts through again,
reminding me of winter, of the
northern harshness, of
steely rocks that never fully thaw.

We dress for the weather
but we are new to town.
Most who have grown acclimated
wear shorts now, and sandals,
and t-shirts, while they smoke cigarettes.

I can't tell if they live in defiance of nature
or if they've simply become part of it.

Insight

Aim to live a small life,
not looking to the vast blue
of the heavenly heights,
nor the churning blue of
the ocean's expanse.

Instead, kneel down
by the daffodils, first
green, then gold, pushing
through the poisoned earth.
They climb past the broken glass,
a shingle, remnants of last year's
water pistol, past the lingering
snow and its coatings of filth.

Aim here, at these small signs.
This is where you'll notice hope,
notice growth, where you'll watch the world
healing itself.

The Cold

Polar Dip

Out of my window I see
winter gray, winter fog,
shades of bark-brown, concrete
glistening, and the deep blue of the hour.

In a little while I will immerse myself in the gray ocean
under leaden skies, sprinkled with flakes
of snow. I will taste
the briny salt and feel the frightening cold.

The moment the icy water envelopes me,
color will rip through my mind,
a kaleidoscope inside, illuminated, bright,
clarity in the aftershocks of pain.

An Apparition

I watched that deer,
that old buck breathing visibly in the autumn cold.
I watched him walk out resolutely from that old Loyalist graveyard.
He was alert.

He strutted across the street in my neighborhood,
where my kids play.
And I watched him from the rearview,
exclaiming all the while:
"Look!"
I said this to my sons in the back seat.

Families walked their dogs
and a couple smoked cigarettes
on the sidewalk
with this magnificent creature in full view.

Some sacrament this is:
The wild of nature passing through the long dead onto the main
road
(they plow it often in the winter)
while I drive my unseemly KIA
listening to podcasts
thinking about the worlds colliding on some strange stage.

The Turning

The chapel is filled with gold,
filtered through the maple
turning outside of the window.

Fall's fading glory is ablaze,
surrendering to the wind-cold
as it reaches its prime.

I can feel the cold against the windowpane,
seeping in like uncomfortable memories.
Is this a chance to heal or be crucified?
To flee or be frozen?

There are not brighter days ahead,
no respite before the full dark closes in.
We are heading toward winter,
toward yellow streetlights on hard concrete
and suppers in the dark.

Autumn Suite

All Souls' Day
The first frost fell last night,
illuminating rooftops and
leaving a little ice at the bottom
of the broken pot that sits
outside our back door.
I looked at it for a moment
in the morning, through the sun-shot
vapor of my breath.
I shivered and returned inside to don
my coat and red toque.

At the other door,
the front door, our pumpkins sag,
wrinkled from the cold. The
black wicks inside them,
are reminders of chocolate bars and
holy saints.

November
We've settled into the winter gray,
the dripping wet before the snow.
All foliage has fallen, save
for the evergreens,
and other conifers that boast of next year's growth.

This dullness hails the Advent fast,
the darkening before the light is lit,
the harbinger of this year's death,
a prophet of the resurrection to come.

A Manifestation
We say the heavens open when
the rain falls
but I wonder why:
The clouds are a covering,
an insulation from the glory
and brilliance
of the sky's blue clarity.

The storm is a shutting that
we call an opening,
a closing we call
a way through.

In the Evening

I heard the whisper of the bare-boned tree
its voice a clatter of naked branches,
skeletal chimes softly drumming
in the night.

I conjure this image before looking, and,
there out my only window, just as I suspected,
I see it:

Ethereal blue bounces off the orb we called the
moon, lightening the darkness
with its reflective luminosity,
an inferior lamp, always giving deference
to the sun.

Ice storm

Fire-flicker and the thunder of falling Ents,
I can make out through the window plum
blossoms enrobed in ice. Our power
is out and with it goes the warmth, save for the
paltry gas fire in our hearth and the heat of
our bodies. We pile up blankets and sleep in one room.

Commuting

In the October light I pedaled over the bridge,
my breath mingling with the vapor on
the river and the tailpipe's exhaust.

I am one with nature,
one with machine, with traffic,
and exploitation.

My gears turn creaking
as I blare my music to
swallow city sounds, concrete sounds,
slack tide slithering out.

October Movement

Wolastoq
Swiftly the river of time carries us along,
like these golden-hued maple leaves
sailing down the river,
down the bountiful river,
during harvest time.

It's autumn now, the first day,
but the summer warmth has returned
unexpectedly, for one last blessing before
the cold clings to stone.

I am in the chapel,
insulated by quiet
while traffic roars outside my window.
The morning light is thick, no longer clear.

I think about my friends,
long drives from here.
And my parents.
This morning's prayer ends in silence.

The Hearth
The wind was brisk this morning
against the concrete and the bridge
over which we drove, blasting heat,
like we did each winter's morning,
a foreboding reminder of what's to come.

In my mind, I entertain images
of soft light,
faces focused and smiling,
eyes meeting one another
without deceit.
The couch is warmed by the fire,
everyone wearing their sweaters.

These scenes with families or friends
are only imaginings,
hopes for holidays and cold weekends off.
They are glimpses of moments in which I can
imagine (remember?)
being present, alive, at ease.

The truth for me has been
tightening days of holding on,
holding it together,
keeping my head down.

Everything Beautiful
This chapel echoes
ticking clock
and muttered prayers,
while through the clear glass I see
the slow decay of vegetable life.

Why is this beautiful to us?
Old churches in the autumn light,
leaves losing their lives in tortured color.

How much peace and coziness
we wring from
the silence of chapels and
the dying of maples leaves.

Left to her own,
Nature brings us this splendid death each year.
We know spring will come,
so we enjoy the arboreal fireworks
while they last.

Old churches are another story.
Though ancient enough to seem
a given,
as being blessedly, always just "there,"
they will crumble and fall like old leaves,
most beautiful before they collapse.
And yet we cannot
count on the same show next year
or the next.

They are beacons,
beautiful,
lost forever from the world.

On the Coast

Today felt like a man whistling a sad song.
I thought this, driving by the canary-colored hill,
and the graveyard misted by the sea.
It was a dark day, even for October.
More wet than cold, foggy, dulling the autumnal leaf-fire.

I ground myself first on the sand, while the mud bowl bay swirls.
I drown out the soothing sounds of nature with podcasts.
(It's better to be productive than to be appreciative.)
After the sand, I climb, into Acadian forest.
I see deer, chipmunks, and some small fowl.
I see expensive raincoats in primary colors,
worn by chubby people who've come to escape the concrete.

The mulch is amber, darkened by the rain.
The trails are like tunnels now, with fallen oak leaves lighting the
way.
They remind me of airplane aisle emergency lights, glowing warm
in a forest of muted green, rock, and moss.

I run here, without sense of time or place, surprised always,
by the rise and the fall of the land.
We've erased topography from our lives,
like we've erased community, and the boundaries of places.

We walk only for exercise, not for the sake of getting where we
need to be.
We drive for comfort, and for speed.

Eucharist in the Snow

The snow is falling heavily
today.
In flakes as light as feathers,
flakes as light as Christ,
on the mount of transfiguration.

In a snow like this,
the world is suspended
in eternity.
Whatever was before, whatever
brokenness or filth, is blanketed
in white.
White shrouds the distances,
dampens sounds and
somehow even stops the chill,
like insulation floating all around.

When we step outside, bundled,
we are conscious of only
ourselves and beauty.
Seeing our breath, hearing
our breath, toques pressed against reddening ears,
feeling the weight of our bodies as our boots crunch,
depressing the snow.

On days like these, work
slows, slackens, and stops.
We stick out our tongues,
to catch intricate patterns

of icy glory, feeling them
sweetly dissolve like that wafer,
the very body of Christ,
turning into liquid,
holy water that flowed from
his side, that flows into us,
in our blood, sustaining us,
and all creatures.

My boys yell in the
backyard, while I pray,
"Oh God, make speed to save us."
I think about the sick,
and dying and all that must be done.

And the snow falls.

Autumn

Pipe smoke and leaf crunch
and that old longing
back again, only broken
by the sun, the warmth
and blue skies now gone.

Still, I am glad to be
alive, for the first time
in nearly four years. I
no longer dread the
morning (though I still
wish I could hasten the night).

The darkness closes early,
dampening life (all of it),
so I lay by candle
flicker and strain my eyes.
Text on a page.
Body in blankets.
Through the window,
soft moon glow.

The Watcher

The spring rain has started falling
in plump, round drops.
These feel icy and glimmer on
the ground,
giving everything a sunless sheen.

It calls to mind
my time at college
walking back and forth
between our apartment and
the lecture hall.
And often to the chapel.

It rained a lot in British Columbia,
in big, globular drops
like those landing on my face,
dripping onto my beard,
this morning.

Back on my college campus,
there was a tree,
a Douglas fir,
towering above all else,
reaching what must be six
or seven stories high.

It looked to belong in
the rain. And sometimes
its branches would wave
in the wind.

It was a sentinel,
a guardian angel.
I thank God for that.
And some mornings like this,
I am sorry to have had
to leave it behind.

The Meaning of a January Snow

The snow freshly fallen
sings its own silent song,
hushing the city sounds,
swaddling concrete echoes
in the softest quiet.

Is this the real, descending as it
does, on the clatter of our lives,
transfiguring our hectic trade,
whitening the stains of oil?

Or is it only a façade?
I have a fear that even
nature's gifts are not powerful enough to
break the black magic of the world.
The filth always finds a way through,
turning the pure flakes to yet another gray.

Outside the Chapel

In the last few days of busyness before the holiness,
there is a freshly fallen blanket of snow.
The feathered crystals are mostly melted with the rise,
rise in temperature.

The snow hushes life,
softens it ever so slightly.
I can still hear motors and
ticking clocks.

The silence I used to crave
now makes me uncomfortable.
I'd rather sit inside by artificial light and
let it snow.

The North

Blinded by the snow,
I see
what's inside of me.
It's not so much who I am
but little gods raging for a voice,
rearing their heads
(and some have more than one).

I speak and the wind sweeps my words away,
carrying them South, away from Arctic ice.

I shiver
and pray.
Shiver, and breathe.
Try to breathe, try to survive.
I build igloos out of water wasted for so many millions of years,
always scarce,
and always bountiful
in some form or another.

I came North to be cold,
to feel the wild groan.
Even here it is hard to find,
vanishing
is everything we thought we knew.
Vanishing is every story we've ever told.

Winter Solstice

My plans fell to the ground
like the needles from the Christmas tree
that we put up earlier than usual
to illuminate the darkness and brighten
the shadows in our thoughts.

We (I) live in shadow now.
Though it's lightening each day
little by little,
my calendar sits empty for weeks at a time.

Stasis, equilibrium, or
perhaps purgatory
(some might call it this).
This is a more hopeful name
because it means it is not the end.

January

In the silent abyss of my life,
I fashion a ladder with a few paltry words,
intending to grasp a rung,
hoping only, as I step, that it leads to someplace solid.

"And the Word was made flesh and dwelt among us."
So it says.
But this word I do not always hear,
this flesh I cannot feel after.

I think the dark leads me here.
It changes nothing, but
veils all that is in a black
velvet shadow,
luxurious, bleak, and
without remorse.

The Fog

A Morning Poem

The echo of brick and tree bone,
asphalt and concrete, is dulled
by the roving mist, which,
blinding the sun, holds close to the river,
following its lead.

I see it spill out onto the bay,
dispersing, like some soul from purgatory
set free.
It too was illumined, not by grace,
but by the earthly light we name
"the day."

Movements in the Fog

1.
Another day of fog,
of beaded water on the window.
Not unpleasant,
but damp, robbing the cool of its charm.

Anxiety is a fog,
creating another mysterious world
out of everyday life,
muddying boundaries and landmarks,
isolating us together.

I thank God when the fog clears.
Things return to how they really are,
instead of how they seem.
Clarity and foresight are restored to mind.

What is a priest for, in all of this?
When most often they are engulfed in the same fog.
What is the Lord calling a priest to do?
To push forward, blind,
or to learn to fall asleep in the fog,
like his Lord slept in the boat caught in the stormy sea?

2.
I woke early in the fog
to take out the garbage at the church.

My sons sprung up with me
while it was still dark.

I grimaced and made coffee.

The aroma of toasted waffles,
the cheap kind, made with buttermilk,
mingled with the cloying scent of children's vitamins
as I opened their lid.

Before morning prayer,
I fill empty stomachs
and do my best to make banter, crusty.

The morning is cool and dark
with light diffused, deadened by cloud.
I'm in the chapel now,
readying myself to pray.

I love this aloneness.
The quiet before the day.
I think about God and life
and worry about my failures.

It's so easy for me to deceive myself.

3.
I hiss fry eggs in my heavy cast iron.
Not hungry, I eat,
though my bowels feel blown up like balloons.
I always feel them inside of me,
pressing, reminding me of the ugliness and filth of excrement.

Looking in the mirror is a relief,
while I brush my teeth.
I'm tired, haggard, even,
but my face is still mine, still human,
still placid, despite the pit-of-stomach dread.

I've long abandoned the hope of prayer in these situations.
Like beads rubbing a groove in my brain,
my prayers never get below the surface.
I say them faithfully.

Each day I force myself out of the door,
like a diver off the edge of a cliff.
I know nothing of the bottom,
only the terror of the fall.

The Fog Again

The fog again -
it hangs late this year,
whitening the air
the way snow whitens the ground.
Separating the city,
it makes neighbors invisible,
softening and dulling all of life.

The fog descends
frequently for all of us
at different times, at different places.
It covers us,
not letting in heaven's light.
Like smoke on the mountain,
it hides God.

I thought I knew the answer to every question,
before I heard the question.
I thought this was faith
but the fog descended and stays still.

Like Smoke

In the early dark,
I sit uncomfortably.
I write nonsense from a broken heart,
a broken body, with nothing left to give,
and eyes focused on the horizon.

I hear (or do I feel?)
the sound of crunching metal.
When little industry is left,
people take what they can get,
destroying garbage with an ocean view.

It's light so little, and
the season has only started.
How does our skin get by with sunless days
and dusky afternoons?

It's supposed to be a beautiful time,
of thanksgiving for God's good gifts.
The problem is that I haven't learned to receive.
I'd rather go back to work and earn my keep.

Everything is hevel,
is vapor and fleeting.
Yet my heart still stirs with visions of meaning
printed down on some pages,
hoping only for a chance to make some connection.

The only answer is onward.
Just pretend there is no one else in the room.
(There isn't)

Dry Spell

I've missed my muse,
whose voice I have not heard
too often
as of late.
Trying to conjure her is no use,
an exercise in
futility.
For when her voice blows into my brain
like some bracing breeze,
I have only to move with the wind.

And when she has hushed,
for me to mime out some dance
as if she were speaking is nothing
more than scampering around like
a rodent who is
at once self-conscious and
completely unaware.

The Home

Birthing Suite

1.
In the hospital harsh light
I think about God.
I'm always thinking about God.
I think about whether I am thinking about God
and whether I'm thinking about him right.

The stillness is clinical
and unsettling, as it should be.
Don't get too comfortable.
Don't stay in that bed too long.

We are waiting, my wife and I.
Waiting for our son to be born,
though he doesn't want to come out.
He doesn't want to squeeze out into the hospital harsh light,
into the cool, sparse air we breathe.

We've been here before.
Twice like this.
Twice, things didn't get this far,
things ending in blood clots and shattered hearts, little bodies
gone limp.

But not today.
Today we hope and anticipate.
Pain is the doorway, not the destination.
It is a door which we can't choose to open, but rather it opens when
it opens,
Providence or something like that.

2.

After birth, everything is a haze of sound
and lights too bright.
To live is to be initiated again
into strangeness, the loudness of the world.

To go out of the door
now takes forethought
and every movement is slowed, like walking under water.

Life has no normal,
no mode of rest.
The truth of life becomes movement, constant movement.

Life becomes:
Hard plastic car seat clips,
warm bodies limp with weariness,
quiet distress over small changes,
bleary-eyed walking with no hope of silence.

This goes on for days, weeks.

Then suddenly,
suddenly,
you find that motion,
the onward push,
has gotten you somewhere.
You realize that you are living,
the way you realize you are riding a bike,
up on two wheels, balancing like you never thought you could.

It's better not to think about how you'll stop,
or how you'll fair when entropy slows you down.

Family Life

The Youngest
He wakes in confusion,
sheet wet with spittle.
He sees dark beyond the wooden
bars that hold him in;
the ceiling is open, as if
it were inviting him to climb.

In a tangle of blankets, he,
gathering himself, sits
and screams.
He knows what he wants to say
but it all comes out as
an indistinct noise.
Pitch and duration are
all that he can control.

The smell of sweat and
urine waft from his heated body.
He hears footsteps on the stairs
and silences.

The Middle
He wakes to sounds of
his brothers' voices, and
sees the dim winter's light.
His bed is damp, he is
damp. His diaper sags and leaks.
Changing his pants, he hides
the evidence and descends,

cloaked in cartoon characters
woven with synthetic threads.

At the table, bleary eyed,
he sits, yawns, and stares into the air.
"Breakfast?" he hears faintly,
as if it were some distant call.
The call repeats.
A glass of water and bowl of
cereal appear before him.

He eats quickly and
disappears into his room,
into a world of castles
and dragons.

The Eldest
His limbs awake before the light of day,
and his eyes snap open in an instant.
The sound of his feet hitting the floor
registers, jolting him further
into consciousness.

He runs, striding into the
dark downstairs, clambering up the
counters. He globs butter
onto an undercooked
waffle and mutters
to himself.

He is furtive in his return to his bedroom
where he feigns waking, calls, whispers,
and calls again the names of his kin.

They awake and he eats again.

On Waking Up

This moment of equilibrium exists,
when I wake, warm, half-covered
in knotted sheets and my eyes
have not yet opened.

I feel the pull of morning,
with its diffuse light pressing
against my eyelids.
The screech of chair legs moving
across the kitchen floor, the
thud and jingle of the cutlery drawers.

And I hear voices.

I rouse myself to the smell
of grain offerings, the roasted
sweetness of brown bread
as it toasts.

On the Failure to Clean Up

When I look out the window to my modest backyard
I see the remnants of a child war:
Upturned pushtoys, shovels strewn,
clumps of dirt cast out of flower beds,
sideways tricycles, and a torn fishing net.
Chaos, brought into ordinary order and
left overnight in answer to calls of "suppertime".

My throat tightens and my muscles tense.
These artifacts from the ruckus are
also the sacraments of
frustrated expectations,
reminders that the world is not mine,
nor mine to control.

Marriage

I'll stick with you
the way yesterday's broccoli
(discarded by my son on the kitchen floor)
sticks to the bottom of my bare foot.

The gel that it makes, when
squished (with rice)
is more effective than many glues,
than the paste we used
when we were children cutting
construction paper.

On Childhood

To my sons, the broken beer bottle
splayed across the trail
has the same allure as luminous sea glass.
They pick up the shards and marvel at their translucence
as if each piece were some heavenly artifact.
They easily overlook the jagged edges
and the malicious intent of whoever
polluted this green pathway to the sea.

I wonder at their wonder,
their (in)ability to appreciate
what the ocean has (not)
transfigured.
Have they some wisdom that I have lost
or is it only a matter of time before
trash loses its lustre?

The End of Our Twenties

We live in a large house with many rooms.
Most of them are empty.
They echo alone when I speak, like these last years of my
twenties.
Tight-knit communities unravel with the passing of kilometres
and years.
Children leech out our energies for one another, leaving our
hearts full,
but with a world-weariness, and an isolation from friends.

I know I'm not alone.

The ache is dull, and at first it comes as a surprise
or a shame
to find oneself walking amidst a lively company,
not noticing as the crowds dwindle in your periphery,
shrinking to a handful
and then you look to find you are walking still
but on your own.

We spread laterally as we age, making ties that bind us
from one another,
but keep us close to those who have almost become parts of
ourselves.
The spacious hours of youth disappear like a smouldering flame.
Now days flick by like trees outside the window of our car.
We focus less on enjoying the drive, and more on the bathroom
stops along the way.
Vending machines and fast-food bring us comfort,

lighting us with their pale, fluorescent light,
and we keep our eyes on our next destination,
never the terminus
(never the terminus!)
We keep moving for fear of death.

White Trash

White is the color of
the toilet paper on the roll
sitting next to the toilet that
is also white.

And white is the trash
down the street, who
comes banging on my front door,
screaming at my wife, frightening
my children, with veins bulging
in his temples.
His white face shades red.
He yells at my wife,
demanding that she give him
money for a coffee, for some dog
food, for a smoke.
"Anything helps," he mutters and yells again
"Change for the bus, even"?

White is the color of Hitler
and his dreams. The latter are whiter
than whitewashed tombs that our brown
Lord referenced when condemning the insincere
religious hypocrites (who were also brown).

Not all whites are Hitler and not all Hitlers are white.
For I have a read a little history and I know Genghis Khan,
Muhammad, and even Joshua wrung blood from
every color of flesh.

On Fatherhood

To be a father is to be angry often
and perplexed beyond measure.

To be a father is to be frustrated
by my own inability to relate
well to my sons, my inability
to lead them in love instead of
pushing them away.

To be a father is to reckon with
my own failure to instill
a love for life and the world,
to help my sons give their lives
for something of value,
and to point toward what this might be.

To be a father is to grieve
the loss of myself,
to grieve the loss of my own
agency, to wake when I wish to,
to think my own thoughts, to
love what I love.

To be a father is to do things that kids like:
McDonald's play places, jungle gyms,
and toy stores,
and to listen to complaints all the while.

To be a father is to suffer in some small way.

Quiet Time

I hear their footfalls
and the rumble of the stairs.

I hide

in my office with my books
and freshly brewed coffee.

We call this "quiet time"
and it seldom lasts long.

I steal away on weekends
and holidays for this
hidden sweetness.

I close the door and hope
for the best,
letting the howls of children
ring out
(at least for a while).
They usually subside
on their own.

Scene from Domestic Life

I cut my neck shaving
and blood poured out,
blood glistened on my skin.
My finger tips were blessed with blood
thinned by water and shave soap.

The cut was deep.
I soaked toilet paper, I
stained my towel, I winced
in the mirror again, and
again, waiting for the blood to stop.

I can't be late for work.

Downstairs, my sons chattered,
seeing with their own eyes
the mortality of their father,
seeping out, soaking paper towel.

My mother-in-law laughed.

My wife spread the band-aid
gingerly, making sure its adhesive
was untouched by my oozing lifeblood.
The wrapper crinkled.
"You are done," she said.
My wound was covered,
held in place until it heals
over long days.

Dreaming on Microfoam

I've forgotten how to live
without another's voice leading me on.
My ribcage has never been so dark.
But tiny voices attached to
clammy hands rouse me from
my slumber.
Their persistence keeps me alive,
if not happy,
if not at peace.

I'd like to carry my pillow with me
like I did in my childhood dreams.
I would pull it out and
slam my head into its softness until
the nightmare turned hazy and I
could leave it behind in quiet sleep.

In the old dreams, my pillow would be
the door to my waking or at least
to a change of scene.
Retreating to its warmth meant
"I am done. I am ready to leave
what is behind."

A Birthday Party

I wish I could forget myself the way
you forget me.

Each winter, the snow covers our paltry lawn
with delicate grace.
Then it melts and seeps and leaks
and is baked into hard ice by the sun.

I see the garish lights,
leftovers from Christmas and
unrealistic expectations.
They've been left to glow forever,
and ever, amen.

The ice-lawn is where we'd
lie to read in August.
We'd listen to music,
watch the clouds, and
smell the sea.

Summer's long forgotten
like my birthday
but I can't forget either
quite so easily.

Waking

When the light has just
begun to waken, to
seep in like ether, and
I am startled by the
smallest voice of all:

I shut my eyes and turn
my head. I force myself back
to dreaming, I try, I awake and
lie perfectly still, ignoring the
pressure on my bladder.

The voice rises and falls and
with it my hope of rest. Before
long, I surrender and rouse myself
to walk toward the stairs.

The Sanctuary

Home Communion

In an old box fitted together
with tongue and groove,
painted red (perhaps
like the pitch ancient Noah used)
I carry gifts:

Silver from the 1930s
(old like my grandmother),
vials of water and wine,
and some wafers, all encased.

Portable holiness, or at least its
accidents, waiting to be
transfigured when words are spoken
like incantations and then I
place the God-life in another's
hands.

Quo Vadis?

I watched the rain wet
the patio stone, enrobing
it with water, slick and
glistening. Dust and grime
darken and turn black, ash-like,
like ash when it is mixed with oil,
smudge-muck, death-dark,
"remember you are dust and to dust
you shall return."

Return.
Return to earth-womb and
its hellish bright center and
then what?
To some memory of an afternoon,
to heavy air and pine-filtered sun,
to lake-shine and dripping feet,
to foot tracks on the trail turning
that dust to mud, darkening it with
sweat and lake water.

Each of the towering trees, pine
and live oak, can be hewn into a
cross. A cross can be carved from their
heartwood, a cross at each one's center.

Mattins

Alone in the chapel again,
I smell dust. I hear
the emptiness of a single ticking clock,
the emptiness of saints and angels
at the throne, invisible,
veiled from the world.

The fog-filtered light
suggests vespers, despite
the early hour.
The dew-soaked cobweb
sags under the weight
of the water of life
while I utter my lonely prayers.

Glossolalia

The incongruence of
word and spirit
of what is spoken and what is felt
jars me back to memories.

I breathe deeply of the fumes
of that old religion,
of air-conditioned buildings,
silk suits, and velvet-bottomed offering plates.
Cloying perfumes hit my nostrils like incense,
mingled with the skunk-scent of stale coffee.

But now I am an outsider in
an unfamiliar guise.
This is how life has changed.

A strange (kind?) man handed me
a gospel tract, and I smiled (beneath my mask).
I slipped out early, into the cold, into my car.
I listened to a podcast while I drove away.

The Stones

The first flurries are falling,
falling slowly.

In the dark of morning,
I reached into my shadow closet
and plucked my wool sweater,
the old one, with snowflakes.

It itches my skin,
even over my clericals.
But it will keep me warm.

Old churches are cold places.
It's as if the foundation stones hold
all bitter memories
and abuses,
keeping them preserved and chilly.

I feel their icy breath on days like these,
their memory of what is forgotten,
of the dead and their displaced city.

The Prayer Bench

Don't fill the silence too quickly.
Let it sit.
Let it age.
Until from it comes some ancient sound,
words wiser than you.

Now pen them down.

Kneel in silence or sit if you must.
The poet's work is prayer work,
a daily office of its own.
Time set apart for
listening and knowing
what you do not know.

Stay silent.

If nothing comes, nothing comes.
Stay a moment longer and then move on.
The night watch isn't long from now.
The morning will follow suit.
The silence will do its work.
It will not return void.

The Fly

In the dewy quiet of mattins
I watched a fly skitter across
the breast of the resurrected Lord.
The sun shone through
his stained-glass skin,
casting the small insect in silhouette.

I got to thinking then
of the flies on dusty Golgotha
partaking of the body
and blood of Christ
(the doctrine of transubstantiation can be
set aside for now).
Here the basest of creation is drawn to
the sickly splatter, warm blood salted
with sweat and fear.

Now I know that it is true:
The heavenly Father feeds the
sparrows while the
thick swarms of cyclorrhapha
sup on the Son.

This dusky Eucharist is a testament
to his depths of love.

The Fraction

Sometimes I wonder what would happen if,
at the moment of the fraction,
a drop of my blood mingled with Christ's.
It would only take a paper cut or
a pin prick: I may not even notice.

Then, one drop of my own life would leak out,
stop, suspended, hanging, only to fall, sending
out ripples in the blood-wine,
wine-blood, his life mixed with mine.

Would I drink it?
I would drink it.

But I could not share it,
from lip to lip, chalice
raised and tipped.

I would hold it back.
"There's too much of me,"
I would think.
Though really, it's only a drop.
It would belong to my Lord only, and
to no one else.

Theology

"Word:"
A sign, pointing to a
reality.
Also, the reality itself,
written down,
between quotation marks.

It is a sign
that is
what it signifies
but
it signifies more than it is.

The Theologian

The poor scholar sits alone,
destitute, save for his hand-me-down tweed
(it must be worth something still).
Such lofty heights for a lonely man,
a doctor that doesn't know how to heal.

Down from his spire
he sees the village church in the valley
with the masses moving this way and that.
He knows they don't know a thing.

But they do know God.
A God who was once among them,
is among them,
patiently loving despite their folly,
despite their grief, their merrymaking.

The scholar is glad to be rid of this lowly God,
glad to be left alone with his thoughts and
books with nobody else above him.

He is close to heaven
but not quite there.
The scholar, the theologian,
is content to be above everybody else.

The Word

I'm an octopus dining by candlelight,
alone, save for the rats under my table
and their horrible words
leaving their filthy lips;
they take on a life of their own.
Utterances brought forth out of the nothingness
of their bellies
to be heard by rotting floorboards
and spores of mold.

"Are they curses or praises?"
I wonder as I feast by firelight.

Some Peace

It's always wrestling and grabbing by the throat.
Taut muscles and sweating flesh
struggling for some unforeseen dawn.

Get on top of life and see who you really are.
Everything inside of you pours out in torrents
like waterfalls,
like rushing waterfalls.

"What are you searching for?" the wise woman asked.

"I guess I am searching for some peace."

Back to the tussle,
back to the grind,
to strong arm and empty heart,
waiting for the unforeseen dawn.

The Good Word

If the Gospel is medicine,
it has to be applied skillfully.
Balm to the broken heart,
broken bones, and tormented mind.
Not to be shouted, but
spoken softly to listening ears.

Did our Lord move about like a clanging symbol,
upsetting tables or upsetting hearts?
Surely; at times he did.
At others, he disappeared into the crowd,
calmed the choppy lake and said,
"Be still."

The frantic hands of the evangelist don't recognize
that they've touched holy things.
Holiness is heavy,
like stone dropped in water.
Fully composed it descends directly without sound.

Enough splashing with holy water
and scripture-citing spittle.
Let us descend slowly,
slowly to our knees,
and in this calm,
preach tidings of peace.

Yellow Oak

The dark and silent chapel wood
finds me here again.
We are strangers,
passing at the bus stop for small talk,
friends along the way.

"Prayer is breathing," I've heard.
I've become accustomed to holding my breath,
or, more hopefully,
I've become so acclimated
to the rhythm of my prayer,
that I no longer am aware of it.

So perhaps prayer is meditation.
It requires moments and balance
and a certain posture.

Or maybe it does not.
In any case, Lord help me pray,
for I can do no good thing without thee.

Yellow Oak (pt. 2)

This silence again in the morning,
the quiet emptiness of wood and glass.
I hear the wind coming through the windows,
the vaulted roof creaks
with groaning too deep for words.

Is this how a church prays unceasingly?

The juxtaposition is jarring.
From screams and shouts at home,
to a quiet day of writing,
deliberate and slow.

The End of Communion

Sometimes I see that I am deceiving myself.
Life spent with geriatric ladies and gentlemen,
navy blue blazers and gold buttons,
calling ourselves "catholic",
passing sandwiches out from behind
locked doors.

Brown skin and white skin
separated roughly under the auspices of the
holy physician, icons long carried away,
we pray to follow his example as he laid
out in his Gospel, that comes before the fourth.

I wear vestments that
cloak my anxious heart, cover my thoughts
of running,
cover trembling ribcage
sick with terror.

I wonder when the roof will fall down.

I wonder too, how long before our Communion
cracks. We've fitted together splinters as best we could,
papered them over with Scripture's rice-paper pages,
reinforced by leaves from journals nobody reads.

www.ingramcontent.com/pod-product-compliance
Lightning Source LLC
LaVergne TN
LVHW051703080426
835511LV00017B/2694